SPELLING for YEAR 8

2,000 WORDS
Every Student Should Know

KS3 English
Ages 12-13

STP

ABOUT THIS BOOK

Using a **fresh approach** to spellings lists, this illustrated collection of Spelling Words is designed **to make spelling fun** for students whilst ensuring they master essential spelling rules by the end of Year 8.

Containing **2,000** carefully selected **level-appropriate** words, this book is made up of **70** Themed Spellings Lists that

- Have **brightly-coloured illustrated backgrounds** and **engaging titles**
- Cover **loads of topics** that **actually interest students** such as social media, photography, and spies
- Relate to other **areas covered at school** including physics, World War I, and figures of speech
- Target **key words that students overuse** (e.g. 'boring', 'lucky', and 'surprised')
- Quietly introduce **specific areas of spelling** that students need to know (e.g. Greek & Latin root words, word building, and homophones & near homophones)
- Are made up of **25 to 30 words each**

HOW TO USE IT

All the **lists are self-contained**, so you can work through them **in order** or, you can dip in to use them for **focused practice**. And, as these lists are themed, they are **also a useful resource** for a range of **writing projects and exercises**.

For your convenience, an **Index** to the **spelling rules, patterns, and themed areas** dealt with by each of the lists is included at the **back of the book** on page 40.

Published by STP Books
An imprint of Swot Tots Publishing Ltd
Kemp House
152-160 City Road
London EC1V 2NX

www.swottotspublishing.com

Text, design, illustrations and layout © Swot Tots Publishing Ltd
First published 2020

Swot Tots Publishing Ltd have asserted their moral right under the Copyright, Designs and Patents Act, 1988, to be identified as the author of this work.

Typeset, cover design, and inside concept design by Swot Tots Publishing Ltd.

British Library Cataloguing-in-Publication Data. A catalogue record for this book is available from the British Library.

ISBN 978-1-912956-33-3

CONTENTS

Silent, But Deadly	5	The Roots Of The Matter I	14
Aaargh!!	5	WWI	14
Luck Of The Draw	6	Ancient History?	15
Happy Endings I	6	Happy Endings II	15
The Play's The Thing	7	Win Some, Lose Some	16
Breaking The Law	7	Head-Scratchers	16
Justice Is Served	8	BOGOF	17
As Dull As Ditchwater	8	Bricks & Mortar	17
Earth-Shattering	9	Mixing Up	18
Be- The Benighted	9	Before...	18
Make An Impact	10	...And After	19
Gee Whiz...	10	Que-ing Up	19
Stop The Presses!	11	Figuratively Speaking...	20
It's Gone Viral	11	Oodles Of Ologies	20
S Is For Surprised	12	Eureka!	21
Applaud, Or Admonish?	12	Bone Idle...Or Not?	21
A Fly In The Ointment	13	Newton's Cradle	22
Making Things Easier	13	Em- Is To Empower	22

CONTENTS Cont.

Double Trouble	23	Rags To Riches	32
Happy Endings III	23	We're Banking On It	32
Claim To Fame	24	A Is For Abecedarian	33
As Wise As An Owl	24	Happy Endings IV	33
Total Bedlam	25	Out Of Sight, Out Of Mind?	34
Going Without	25	Say Cheese!	34
Short & Sweet	26	C-eeing Double	35
Long-winded	26	I Don't Feel So Good	35
Wunderbar!	27	A Rapid Rise...	36
That Said...	27	...Or A Slow Decline?	36
The Roots Of The Matter II	28	The Roots Of The Matter III	37
Munificent, Or Miserly?	28	Happy Endings V	37
Hue & Cry!	29	Above Or Below Par?	38
T Is For Trickery	29	Body Language	38
That Doesn't Look Right...	30	HOW Do You Say That?!	39
Overt Vs Covert	30	That's A Proper Word?!	39
James Bond & Co.	31		
Politically Correct?	31	Index	40

Silent, But Deadly

aplomb	knick-knack	resuscitate
ascetic	malign	ricochet
champagne	miscellaneous	scenic
consignment	mnemonic	scimitar
czar	nascent	sepulchre
ensign	overwrought	succumb
exhortation	phlegm	synchronous
indictment	psychedelic	thumbscrew
jostle	rapport	whorl
kitsch	rescind	writhed

Aaargh!!

acrophobia	germophobia	pyrophobia
aerophobia	gynophobia	technophobia
agoraphobia	hydrophobia	toxiphobia
ailurophobia	necrophobia	xenophobia
anemophobia	neophobia	zoophobia
aquaphobia	panophobia	
arachnophobia	pathophobia	
biophobia	phagophobia	
chemophobia	philosophobia	
claustrophobia	photophobia	

Luck Of The Draw

chance
coincidental
destined
felicitous
fluky
fortuitous
fortunate
heaven-sent
karmic
opportune

propitious
providential
serendipitous
unforeseen
unlooked-for
accursed
adverse
calamitous
catastrophic
doomed

hapless
ill-fated
ill-starred
infelicitous
jinxed
luckless
ominous
star-crossed
unfavourable
unfortunate

Happy Endings I

apprenticeship
assistantship
authorship
bipartisanship
censorship
championship
courtship
dictatorship
fellowship
friendship

hardship
internship
kinship
leadership
membership
ownership
partnership
penmanship
premiership
professorship

readership
scholarship
showmanship
statesmanship
workmanship

The Play's The Thing

act
apron
aside
audition
backstage
box office
callback
cast
company
costumes

cues
curtain call
dialogue
downstage
dramatis personae
dress rehearsal
front of house
interval
matinee
monologue

offstage
playwright
props
proscenium arch
scenery
scene
soliloquy
thespian
understudy
upstage

Breaking The Law

abductor
abettor
arsonist
assassin
burglar
cat burglar
confidence trickster
cybercriminal
embezzler
fraudster

gangster
gunrunner
hijacker
kidnapper
mugger
murderer
phone hacker
pickpocket
poacher
smuggler

stalker
terrorist
trafficker
trespasser
vandal

Justice Is Served

accusation	hearsay	prosecutor
advocate	imprisonment	punishment
arbitrator	incarceration	rehabilitation
bailiff	innocence	sentence
conviction	jury	verdict
defendant	justice	
deterrent	litigator	
dock	magistrate	
expert witness	offence	
guilt	penalty	

As Dull As Ditchwater

banal	lifeless	tedious
bland	mind-numbing	undramatic
boring	monotonous	uneventful
drab	pedestrian	unexciting
dreary	ponderous	unimaginative
dry	prosaic	uninspiring
dull	stale	uninteresting
humdrum	stodgy	unsensational
insipid	stuffy	unspectacular
leaden	suspenseless	vapid

Earth-Shattering

active fault
aftershock
bedrock
cataclysm
core
crust
damage
destruction
epicentre
geology

geophysics
hertz
injury
intensity
landslide
magnitude
mainshock
mantle
recurrence
Richter scale

rubble
seismic
seismograph
seismology
shock wave
survivor
tectonic
trapped
tremor
upheaval

Be- The Benighted

befit
befriend
beguile
behead
belabour
belie
belittle
bemire
bemoan
bemuse

beseem
besiege
besmirch
bespeak
bestride
betide
betoken
betroth
bewail
bewitch

becalmed
bedecked
befitting
befuddled
bejewelled
benighted
beribboned
besotted
bespoke
bewigged

Make An Impact

Armageddon	audacious	alluring
bloodbath	beauteous	beguiled
doom	breathtaking	charismatically
insidious	celebratory	compelled
reckoning	colossal	deliriously
lurking	defiantly	enticingly
nightmarish	effortlessly	hypnotic
perilous	flawless	riveting
plunged	thwarted	tantalize
shattering	vanquish	unabashed

Gee Whiz...

aggrandise	doggerel	sniggered
aggravation	haggard	staggering
aggregate	juggling	suggestive
aggression	laggard	swaggered
aggrieved	loggerhead	thuggee
arpeggios	niggles	thuggery
bedraggled	nugget	toboggan
braggadocio	piggyback	toggle
braggarts	sluggard	trigger
doggedly	smuggled	ziggurat

Stop The Presses!

broadsheet	headline	redaction
byline	journalist	reporter
column	layout	retraction
copywriter	misquotation	source
distribution	objectivity	strapline
editor	paragraphing	subeditor
editorial	photojournalist	subscribers
fact-checking	proofreading	tabloid
font	quotations	typesetting
fourth estate	quote	typography

It's Gone Viral

algorithm	dashboard	hashtag
analytics	direct message	impressions
archiving	emoji	influencer
avatar	engagement	live stream
bitmoji	favourite	mention
block	feed	metric
boosted post	filter	notification
caption	followers	platform
clickbait	geotag	repost
crowdsourcing	handle	thread

S Is For Surprised

agape	floored	stunned
amazed	flummoxed	stupefied
astonished	goggle-eyed	taken aback
astounded	jolted	thunderstruck
benumbed	nonplussed	wide-eyed
confounded	shell-shocked	
dazed	shocked	
dumbfounded	speechless	
dumbstruck	staggered	
flabbergasted	startled	

Applaud, Or Admonish?

acclaim	laud	chide
adulate	praise	condemn
applaud	revere	criticise
celebrate	salute	lecture
commend	venerate	rebuke
compliment	admonish	reprehend
congratulate	berate	reprimand
extol	castigate	reproach
hail	censure	scold
honour	chastise	upbraid

A Fly In The Ointment

barrier	hindrance	restriction
brick wall	hitch	setback
complication	hold-up	snag
constraint	hurdle	stonewall
curb	impediment	stoppage
deterrence	limitation	
drawback	mishap	
embargo	obstacle	
encumbrance	obstruction	
handicap	restraint	

Making Things Easier

accelerating	furtherance	promotion
advancement	galvanization	spur
assistance	goad	stimulant
backing	impetus	stimulation
easing	incentive	stimulus
enablement	inducement	
encouragement	instigation	
expedition	invitation	
facilitation	momentum	
fostering	motivation	

The Roots Of The Matter I

hyperacidity	hypertensive	hypomania
hyperactive	hypertext	hyponym
hyperbola	hyperthermia	hypostasis
hyperbolic	hyperventilate	hypotaxis
hypercritical	hypoallergenic	hypotensive
hyperinflation	hypochondria	hypotenuse
hyperkinetic	hypocrisy	hypothermia
hyperlink	hypocritical	hypothesize
hypersensitive	hypodermic	hypothetical
hypersonic	hypoglycaemic	hypoxic

WWI

Allies	draft	machine gun
armistice	dreadnought	mobilization
artillery	entente	munitions
assassination	front	nationalism
casualties	gas mask	No Man's Land
conscription	Great War	pacifist
contraband	home front	propaganda
convoy	infantry	treaty
counter-attack	land mine	trench warfare
doughboy	League of Nations	U-boat

Ancient History?

archivist	predecessor	Victorian
digitization	regnal year	Enlightenment
documentation	repository	Interregnum
dynastic	Caroline	Protectorate
genealogy	Edwardian	Regency
heritage	Elizabethan	colonialism
historiographer	Georgian	imperialism
historiography	Henrician	industrialisation
lineage	Jacobean	modernism
memorabilia	Marian	postmodernism

Happy Endings II

auctioneer	muleteer	rocketeer
balladeer	munitioneer	scrutineer
buccaneer	musketeer	sloganeer
charioteer	mutineer	sonneteer
electioneer	orienteer	volunteer
engineer	pamphleteer	
gazetteer	privateer	
leafleteer	profiteer	
marketeer	puppeteer	
mountaineer	racketeer	

Win Some, Lose Some

advantageous	remunerative	dissipated
booming	rewarding	failed
enriching	successful	forfeited
flourishing	thriving	gambled
fruitful	worthwhile	impoverished
gainful	deficient	indebted
lucrative	depleted	penalised
productive	deprived	ruined
profitable	destitute	squandered
prosperous	dispossessed	unprofitable

Head-Scratchers

auger	ewe	mean
augur	yew	mien
baize	faun	rota
bays	fawn	rotor
censer	gild	satire
censor	guild	satyr
cite	hoard	throes
site	horde	throws
discreet	laps	vale
discrete	lapse	veil

BOGOF

advertorial	flyer	publicist
billboard	FOMO	publicity
blurb	handout	sandwich board
boost	infomercial	slogan
brochure	introductory offers	special offers
campaign	jingle	
circular	launch	
commercials	logo	
discounting	placard	
endorsement	promotional	

Bricks & Mortar

brickwork	fascia	planking
building site	fenestration	planning permission
catwalk	foundation	reconstruction
cladding	infrastructure	refurbishment
construction	installation	renovation
demolition	insulation	restoration
development	maintenance	roofing
double glazing	masonry	scaffolding
edifice	new-build	self-build
fabrication	partition	superstructure

Mixing Up

absorb	commingle	link
ally	converge	marry
amalgamate	fuse	meld
assimilate	incorporate	merge
blend	integrate	mingle
cement	intermingle	pool
coalesce	intermix	synthesise
combine	join	unify
conflate	knit	unite
congregate	liaise	yoke

Before...

ancestor	herald	prefix
antecedent	overture	preliminary
antedate	pioneer	prelude
anticipate	preamble	premature
beforehand	precede	premonition
curtain-raiser	precedent	presentiment
foregoing	precursor	previous
forerunner	predate	prior
foreshadow	pre-existing	prologue
foretaste	preface	usher

...And After

afterwards	ensuing	postscript
belated	epilogue	progeny
closing	eventual	rearmost
concluding	hindmost	resultant
consequent	hindsight	subsequent
crowning	latter	succeeding
deferment	posterity	successive
deferral	posthumous	successor
descendant	post-mortem	terminating
endmost	postponement	ultimate

Que-ing Up

appliqué	discotheque	physique
arabesque	goblinesque	picaresque
baroque	grotesque	picturesque
barque	macaque	pique
bisque	marque	plaque
boutique	masque	risqué
burlesque	mosque	statuesque
calque	mystique	technique
communiqué	oblique	torque
critique	opaque	unique

Figuratively Speaking...

allegory	dramatic irony	paradox
alliteration	euphemism	pathetic fallacy
allusion	figure of speech	pathos
anaphora	hyperbole	personification
antithesis	irony	pun
apostrophe	metaphor	sibilance
assonance	metonymy	simile
aural imagery	motif	symbol
bathos	onomatopoeia	synecdoche
contrast	oxymoron	visual imagery

Oodles Of Ologies

angelology	ecology	oceanology
anthropology	Egyptology	oncology
bacteriology	etymology	ophthalmology
biotechnology	graphology	ornithology
cardiology	histology	palaeontology
cosmology	hydrology	pharmacology
criminology	meteorology	philology
cryptology	microbiology	theology
demonology	mineralogy	toxicology
dermatology	musicology	vulcanology

Eureka!

abstraction
concept
conception
impression
notion
preconception
cognition
observation
perception
reflection

conclusion
conviction
conjecture
deduction
guess
hunch
hypothesis
speculation
supposition
theory

brainchild
brainstorm
brainwave
inspiration
formulation

BONE IDLE...OR NOT?

apathetic
indolent
inert
lackadaisical
languid
languorous
lethargic
loafing
phlegmatic
shiftless

slothful
sluggish
spiritless
stolid
work-shy
active
animated
assiduous
conscientious
diligent

dynamic
energetic
indefatigable
industrious
inventive
operative
painstaking
persevering
persistent
tireless

Newton's Cradle

alternating current	conductor	frequency
ampere	convection	half-life
antimatter	decibel	joule
atom	density	newton
calorie	diffraction	particle
cathode ray	diffusion	proton
centre of gravity	diode	refraction
centrifugal force	direct current	resistance
centripetal force	electron	spectrum
charge	fission	velocity

Em- Is To Empower

emaciate	embezzle	empathise
emanate	embitter	empeople
emancipate	emblaze	empower
emasculate	emblazon	empurple
embalm	embody	emulsify
embank	embolden	
embark	emboss	
embattle	embower	
embed	embroil	
embellish	empanel	

DOUBLE TROUBLE

allocation

embellishment

hallucination

intelligentsia

malleable

asymmetric

commercialise

commiserate

consummate

mammalian

apportion

inopportune

puppetry

supplicant

Zeppelin

aberration

catarrh

corrugated

extracurricular

surreptitiously

assassinate

connoisseur

disseminate

percussionist

quintessential

attenuate

bloodletting

gluttonous

guttural

intermittency

Happy Endings III

adventuresome

bothersome

burdensome

cuddlesome

cumbersome

fearsome

flavoursome

frolicsome

gamesome

gladsome

gruesome

irksome

lithesome

loathsome

meddlesome

quarrelsome

tiresome

toothsome

twosome

unwholesome

venturesome

wearisome

wholesome

winsome

worrisome

Claim To Fame

acclaimed

celebrated

distinguished

eminent

esteemed

exalted

illustrious

leading

legendary

pre-eminent

prominent

remarkable

renowned

reputable

respected

delinquent

discreditable

disgraceful

dishonourable

disreputable

ignominious

iniquitous

louche

nefarious

notorious

opprobrious

scandalous

shady

shameful

troublesome

As Wise As An Owl

acuity

acumen

acuteness

astuteness

canniness

circumspection

clear-sightedness

cleverness

discernment

enlightenment

insight

judgement

judiciousness

keenness

perceptiveness

perspicacity

prudence

sagaciousness

sagacity

sageness

sapience

savviness

sharpness

sharp-wittedness

shrewdness

Total Bedlam

anarchy
bedlam
chaos
commotion
confusion
crisis
disarray
disorder
disorderliness
fiasco

furore
havoc
jumble
maelstrom
mayhem
misorder
misrule
muddle
pandemonium
panic

rampage
riot
shambles
tumult
turbulence
turmoil
unrest
uproar
vortex
whirl

Going Without

aridity
barrenness
blight
calamity
catastrophe
dearth
deprivation
destitution
drought
emergency

famish
insufficiency
lack
meagreness
paucity
pestilence
poverty
predicament
privation
ravagement

scarcity
severity
shortage
sparsity
starvation
straits
strife
suffering
undersupply
want

SHORT & SWEET

abbreviated
abridged
aphoristic
apposite
compact
compendious
compressed
concise
condensed
contracted

curtailed
economical
encapsulated
essential
incisive
laconic
monosyllabic
pertinent
pithy
relevant

shortened
succinct
summarised
telegraphic
truncated

Long-winded

circuitous
circumlocutory
diffuse
digressive
discursive
embellished
embroidered
expansive
garrulous
inflated

interminable
lengthy
loquacious
meandering
profuse
prolix
protracted
rambling
repetitious
roundabout

substantial
tortuous
verbose
voluble
wordy

WUNDERBAR!

abseil	eiderdown	putsch
angst	Gesundheit	rucksack
bagel	haversack	schadenfreude
Bauhaus	kaput	spiel
Bildungsroman	leitmotif	spritz
blitzkrieg	muesli	uber-
cobalt	Neanderthal	waltz
dachshund	poltergeist	wanderlust
delicatessen	prattle	wunderkind
doppelgänger	pretzel	zeitgeist

That Said...

above all	in practice	namely
admittedly	in retrospect	notably
all told	in short	notwithstanding
by the same token	in sum	on balance
completely	in the first place	on the whole
contrastingly	in theory	overall
conversely	inasmuch as	regardless
hence	insofar as	undoubtedly
in all	lest	whereas
in contrast	likewise	wholly

The Roots Of The Matter II

interactive
interdepartmental
interfacial
intergalactic
interknitted
interlaced
interlinear
interlingual
interlining
interlocking

intermedial
interpersonal
intertextual
interwoven
intra-abdominal
intracellular
intracranial
intradermal
intramolecular
intramural

intramuscular
intravenous
introduction
introspective
introverted

Munificent, Or Miserly?

altruistic
ample
bountiful
charitable
copious
fulsome
lavish
liberal
magnanimous
munificent

philanthropic
plentiful
unselfish
unsparing
unstinting
begrudging
close-fisted
economical
frugal
meagre

miserly
parsimonious
penny-pinching
penurious
prudent
scanty
spartan
stingy
thrifty
tight-fisted

HUE & CRY!

babel
ballyhoo
brouhaha
cacophony
clamour
clangour
cri de cœur
demurral
denunciation
disputation

dissent
eruption
ferment
fracas
hubbub
hullabaloo
outburst
outcry
protestation
racket

remonstrance
ruckus
rumpus
unquietness
vociferation

T Is For Trickery

artifice
betrayal
chicanery
covertness
cozenage
cunning
deception
dissembling
dissimulation
double-dealing

duplicity
evasion
falsehood
fraudulence
furtiveness
guile
guilefulness
intrigue
machination
mendacity

obliquity
oiliness
shiftiness
skulduggery
slipperiness
smokescreen
stratagem
subterfuge
swindling
treachery

That Doesn't Look Right...

allegiance	harass	perseverance
atheist	humorous	personnel
camouflage	idiosyncrasy	Portuguese
Caribbean	indict	pronunciation
chauffeur	inoculate	quarantine
colleague	kernel	reference
concede	millennium	supersede
dilemma	omission	upholstery
exhilarate	outrageous	welfare
gauge	pavilion	withhold

OVERT VS COVERT

above-board	plain-spoken	enigmatic
acknowledged	straightforward	furtive
avowed	undisguised	implicit
candid	unguarded	secluded
evident	unreserved	secreted
forthright	camouflaged	sneaky
frank	clandestine	subterranean
obvious	classified	surreptitious
outspoken	confidential	unadvertised
overt	covert	underhand

James Bond & Co.

cipher
concealment
conspiracies
counter-espionage
counterfeiting
counter-intelligence
cryptography
deceit
decoding
disguise

encryption
espionage
forgery
handler
infiltration
insider
intelligence
interception
interrogation
mole

reconnaissance
recruitment
sabotage
safe house
secret service
shadowing
stealth
subversion
undercover
underground

Politically Correct?

absolutism
abdication
accession
annexation
autocrat
banishment
claimant
coercion
conspiracy
cult

declaration
decree
despotism
domination
exile
invasion
monocracy
monocrat
occupation
oligarchy

oppression
potentate
revolution
secession
succession
supremacy
totalitarianism
unanimity
unification
usurpation

Rags To Riches

bankrupt	needy	flush
beggared	pauperised	loaded
bereft	penniless	moneyed
broke	poverty-stricken	privileged
cash-strapped	skint	propertied
distressed	straitened	prospering
impecunious	threadbare	replete
indigent	underprivileged	well heeled
insolvent	affluent	well off
necessitous	advantaged	well-to-do

We're Banking On It

account	debit	overdraft
asset	deposit	pay cheque
banking	equity	regulator
budget	foreign exchange	reserve
capital	income	revenue
cashier	interest	savings account
cashpoint	investment	statement
credit	liability	teller
currency	mortgage	transaction
current account	offshore	withdrawal

A Is For Abecedarian

abecedarian
antiquarian
apiarian
Aquarian
authoritarian
barbarian
disciplinarian
egalitarian
equalitarian
grammarian

hereditarian
humanitarian
libertarian
librarian
millenarian
parliamentarian
pescatarian
predestinarian
proletarian
sectarian

seminarian
totalitarian
utilitarian
vegetarian
veterinarian

HAPPY ENDINGS IV

agelessness
aimlessness
artlessness
bottomlessness
boundlessness
breathlessness
carelessness
cluelessness
effortlessness
endlessness

facelessness
faithlessness
faultlessness
fearlessness
flawlessness
guiltlessness
harmlessness
heartlessness
homelessness
lawlessness

mercilessness
pitilessness
mindlessness
recklessness
relentlessness
remorselessness
ruthlessness
selflessness
thoughtlessness
weightlessness

Out Of Sight, Out Of Mind?

awareness
cognisance
contemplation
memorials
memory
mindfulness
nostalgia
recall
recollection
remembrance

reminiscence
retrospection
absent-mindedness
absorption
amnesia
forgetfulness
inattention
inattentiveness
incognisance
obliteration

oblivion
obliviousness
overlooking
repression
unawareness

Say Cheese!

aperture
camera obscura
camera-shy
capture
close-up
contact sheet
darkroom
digital camera
exposure
flash

flashbulb
focal length
foreground
frame
ghosting
grain
high-resolution
low-resolution
negative
optical zoom

overexposure
photobombing
photogenic
photo shoot
pinhole camera
projection
red-eye
selfie
sepia
snapshot

C-eeing Double

accede
accentuate
accessory
accidental
accelerant
acclimatise
accolade
baccalaureate
bacchanalian
desiccated

eccentricity
ecclesiastical
fettuccine
Fibonacci
flaccid
impeccably
inaccuracies
occasioned
Occident
occlude

occult
occupancy
saccharine
staccato
stuccoed
succinctly
succour
succulent
succumbing
vaccinate

I Don't Feel So Good

anorexia
appendicitis
arthritis
bronchitis
bulimia
chickenpox
cholera
common cold
diabetes
dysentery

gout
hepatitis
hypertension
influenza
leprosy
malaria
measles
meningitis
mumps
pneumonia

polio
rabies
rheumatism
salmonella
sciatica
shingles
tuberculosis
typhoid fever
whooping cough
yellow fever

A Rapid Rise...

accelerate
accumulate
amplify
appreciate
ascend
aspire
burgeon
elevate
enlarge
escalate

exacerbate
expand
extend
heighten
improve
intensify
mount
multiply
mushroom
proliferate

promote
redouble
skyrocket
snowball
soar
surge
uplift
uprear
upturn
wax

...OR A SLOW DECLINE?

abate
collapse
compress
contract
debase
decimate
decline
de-escalate
deflate
degenerate

demote
deplete
depreciate
deteriorate
devolve
diminish
downscale
downsize
dwindle
ebb

plummet
plunge
recede
reduce
relax
shrink
slump
subside
tumble
wane

The Roots Of The Matter III

benediction
benedictory
benefactor
benefactress
beneficence
beneficial
beneficiary
benefit
benevolence
benign

benison
maladapted
maladjusted
maladministration
malady
malaise
malcontent
malediction
malefactor
malfeasance

malformed
malice
malignant
malnutrition
malodorous

Happy Endings V

analgesic
antagonistic
chimeric
didactic
eclectic
elliptic
empathetic
gastronomic
hydraulic
idiosyncratic

impressionistic
kinetic
neurotic
opportunistic
peripatetic
philharmonic
pluralistic
problematic
quadraphonic
quixotic

rhapsodic
ritualistic
sardonic
soporific
sporadic
stoic
symptomatic
systemic
talismanic
therapeutic

Above Or Below Par?

adept	scholar	freshman
authority	specialist	hobbyist
expert	virtuoso	inexpert
fiend	whiz	initiate
maestro	wizard	Jack-of-all-trades
master	amateur	layperson
professional	apprentice	neophyte
proficient	dabbler	non-professional
pundit	dilettante	novice
savant	fledgling	tinkerer

BODY LANGUAGE

abdomen	cranium	spinal cord
aorta	diaphragm	spleen
appendix	gall bladder	tendons
arteries	larynx	thyroid
bone marrow	ligaments	tonsils
bronchi	lymph nodes	torso
capillaries	oesophagus	trachea
cartilage	pancreas	veins
cerebrum	pharynx	ventricle
circulation	sinews	vertebrae

HOW DO YOU SAY THAT?!

adolescence	foyer	peremptory
aegis	glower	regime
annals	gyro	rendezvous
awry	macabre	sergeant
brooch	mascarpone	sherbet
cache	mauve	sorbet
crinoline	meme	statistics
dishabille	meringue	wrath
espresso	moniker	wreath
flautist	niche	wyvern

THAT'S A PROPER WORD?!

balderdash	gewgaw	namby-pamby
bamboozle	gobsmacked	nincompoop
bombastic	hotchpotch	pernickety
bossyboots	kerfuffle	quicksilver
caboodle	killjoy	razzmatazz
codswallop	kowtow	shebang
filibuster	petrolhead	shenanigans
fisticuffs	lugubrious	switcheroo
flibbertigibbet	mishmash	titbit
flummox	murmuration	whirligig

INDEX

In the following entries, the letter 'A' refers to the upper list on the page, while 'B' refers to the lower one.

ENGLISH LANGUAGE CURRICULUM-BASED WORDS

Commonly Mispronounced Words (p. 39: A)

Commonly Mistaken Spellings (p. 30: A)

Double Consonants (p. 23: A)

German Loanwords (p. 27: A)

Homophones & Near Homophones (p. 16: B)

Letter Strings
Verbs Beginning with 'em-' (p. 22: B)
Words Containing 'cc' (p. 35: A)
Words Containing 'gg' (p. 10: B)
Words Ending in 'que' (p. 19: B)

Prefixes
be- (p. 9: B)

Prefixes/Word Roots
hyper- & hypo- (p. 14: A)
inter- intra- intro- (p. 28: A)

Silent Letters (p. 5: A)

Suffixes
-ic (p. 37: B)

Suffixes/Word Building
-arian (p. 33: A)
-eer (p. 15: B)
-lessness (p. 33: B)
-ship (p. 6: B)
-some (p. 23: B)

Word Roots
ben/e & mal/e (p. 37: A)

ENGLISH LITERATURE CURRICULUM-BASED WORDS
Figures of Speech (p. 20: A)
Words & Phrases for Formal Writing (p. 27: B)

GENERAL KNOWLEDGE WORDS
Advertising (p. 17: A)
Banking (p. 32: B)
Body, The (p. 38: B)
Buildings & Construction (p. 17: B)
Diseases (p. 35: B)
Earthquakes (p. 9: A)
Famine (p. 25: B)
History Terms (p. 15: A)
Law Breakers (p. 7: B)
Law Courts (p. 8: A)
Newspapers (p. 11: A)
Phobias (p. 5: B)
Photography (p. 34: B)
Physics (p. 22: A)
Political Power (p. 31: B)
Social Media (p. 11: B)
Spies & Espionage (p. 31: A)
Theatre, The (p. 7: A)
World War I (p. 14: B)
'Ology' Words (p. 20: B)

ANTONYM PAIRS
Active vs Inactive (p. 21: B)
Applause vs Admonition (p. 12: B)
Expert vs Novice (p. 38: A)
Gain vs Loss (p. 16: A)
Generous vs Miserly (p. 28: B)
Lucky vs Unlucky (p. 6: A)
Overt vs Covert (p. 30: B)
Poverty vs Wealth (p. 32: A)
Remembered vs Forgotten (p. 34: A)

SYNONYMS
Boring (p. 8: B)
Surprised (p. 12: A)

WORD CLUSTERS
After (p. 19: A)
Before (p. 18: B)
Chaos (p. 25: A)
Digression (p. 26: B)
Down (p. 36: B)
Exactness (p. 26: A)
Facilitation (p. 13: B)
Idea (p. 21: A)
Mix (p. 18: A)
Obstruction (p. 13: A)
Outcry (p. 29: A)
Trickery (p. 29: B)
Up (p. 36: A)
Wisdom (p. 24: B)

CREATIVE WRITING WORDS
Fun Words (p. 39: B)

Good Reputation vs Bad Reputation (p. 24: A)

Power Words (p. 10: A)

Printed in Great Britain
by Amazon